ABC Book For Preschool Kids

Name: ________________________

Published by KBPublication
Text copyright © **Khyati Banker, 2024.**

 A catalogue record for this book is available from the National Library of Australia

National Library of Australia Cataloguing-in-Publication entry
Author: Khyati Banker, author.
Title: ABC for Preschool Kids
By Khyati Banker;
ISBN: 978-1-7635491-2-8
Target Audience: For Preschool age.

A For Ape

A for Albatross

A For Aqua

B for Bear

B for Bluebird

B for Blue

C for Cat

C for Crow

C for Cream

D for Dog

D for Dove

D for Dark Blue

E for Elephant

E for Eagle

E for Emerald

F for Fox

F for Flamingo

F for Fuchsia

G for Giraffe

G for Gull

G for Green

H for Horse

H for Hummingbird

H for Hazel

I for Indri

I for Ibis

I for Ivory

J for Jackal

J for Blue Jay

J for Jasmine

K for Kangaroo

K for KIWI

K for Kumquat

L for Lion

L for Lovebird

L for Lavender

M for Monkey

M for Magpie

M for Magenta

N for Numbat

N for Nightingale

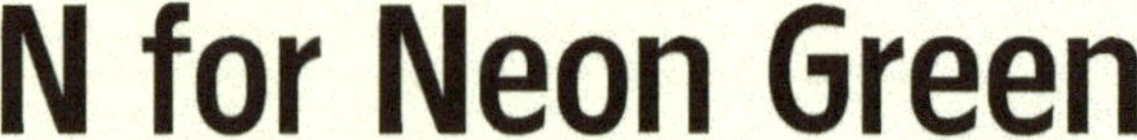

N for Neon Green

O for Otter

O for Ostrich

O for Orange

P for Penguin

P for Parrot

P for Purple

Q for Quoll

Q for Quail

Q for Quartz Pink

R for Rabbit

R for Robin

R for Red

S for Squirrel

S for Sparrow

S for Silver

T for Tiger

T for Toucan

T for Tangerine

U for Uakari

U for Ultramarine Flycatcher

U for Umber

V for Vole

V for Vulture

V for Violet

W for Wolf

W for Woodpecker

W for White

X for Xerus

X for Xantus's Hummingbird

X for Xanthic

Y for Yak

Y for Yellowhammer

Y for Yellow

Z for Zebra

Z for Zebra Dove

Z for Zaffre